THE
POWER
OF RELENTLESS PRAYER AND RESILIENT FAITH

PRAYER LAB JOURNAL

DORIS E. GOLDER

THIS JOURNAL BELONGS TO

NAME _____

ADDRESS _____

_____

PHONE _____

EMAIL _____

MEMO _____

_____

_____

The Power of Relentless Prayer and Resilient Faith Prayer LAB Journal by Doris E. Golder

Published by D'Vine Strategies LLC
PO Box 20052
Indianapolis, IN 46220

This book or parts thereof may not be reproduced in any form, stored in a retrieval system, or transmitted in any form by any means—electronic, mechanical, photocopy, recording, or otherwise—without prior written permission of the publisher, except as provided by United States of America copyright law.

Unless otherwise noted, all Scripture quotations are taken from the King James Version of the Bible.

Scripture quotations marked AMP are from the Amplified Bible. Copyright © 2015 by The Lockman Foundation, La Habra, CA 90631. All rights reserved. Used by permission.

Scripture quotations marked CSB have been taken from the Christian Standard Bible®, Copyright © 2017 by Holman Bible Publishers. Used by permission. Christian Standard Bible® and CSB® are federally registered trademarks of Holman Bible Publishers.

Scripture quotations marked NIV are taken from the Holy Bible, New International Version®, NIV®. Copyright © 1973, 1978, 1984, 2011 by Biblica, Inc.™ Used by permission of Zondervan. All rights reserved worldwide. www.zondervan.com. The "NIV" and "New International Version" are trademarks registered in the United States Patent and Trademark Office by Biblica, Inc.™

Scripture quotations marked NKJV are taken from the New King James Version®. Copyright © 1982 by Thomas Nelson. Used by permission. All rights reserved.

Scripture quotations marked NLT are from the Holy Bible, New Living Translation, copyright © 1996, 2004, 2007. Used by permission of Tyndale House Publishers, Inc., Wheaton, IL 60189. All rights reserved.

Scripture quotations marked THE MESSAGE are from *The Message: The Bible in Contemporary English*, copyright © 1993, 1994, 1995, 1996, 2000, 2001, 2002. Used by permission of NavPress Publishing Group.

Copyright © 2024 by Doris E. Golder
All rights reserved

Visit the author's website at www.dvinestrategies.com.

International Standard Book Number: 978-1-7338534-4-6

While the author has made every effort to provide accurate internet addresses at the time of publication, neither the publisher nor the author assumes any responsibility for errors or for changes that occur after publication. Further, the publisher does not have any control over and does not assume any responsibility for author or third-party websites or their content.

Please note: This Prayer Lab Journal is only a tool to use to write your thoughts, comments, and reflections along with God's promises to meditate on daily as you wait to hear from Him. If you need additional help in working through life or medical challenges, we encourage you to seek the advice of a spiritual adviser or medical provider.

The author's photo by: Haley Rose Photography

24 25 26 27 28 — 9 8 7 6 5 4 3 2 1

Printed in the United States of America

CONTENTS

INTRODUCTION: WHY A PRAYER LAB JOURNAL...................ix

1. PRAYER LAB REFRESHER........... 1
2. PRAYER REQUESTS................. 6
3. GUIDED PRAYER FOCUSES........ 32
4. WHILE YOU ARE WAITING........ 64
5. REFLECTIVE MOMENTS OF THE SOUL..................... 72
6. FASTING: TAKING YOUR PRAYERS TO THE NEXT LEVEL.............. 80
7. ANSWERED PRAYERS 85

A SPECIAL NOTE FROM THE AUTHOR................... 100

Introduction
WHY A PRAYER LAB JOURNAL

THE POWER OF Relentless Prayer and Resilient Faith Prayer LAB Journal is designed to help you keep your thoughts, ideas, prayer petitions, and more in one safe place. This journal is a companion guide with the paperback titled *The Power of Relentless Prayer and Resilient Faith.*

The Master will commune with you in various ways. You may hear a still, small voice speak within or a gentle prompting to move forward or to sit still or even receive a (comforting or enlightening) word as you read and mediate on His Word daily.

As you began your prayer journey, infuse the three elements of prayer together found in the Prayer Lab in chapter 5 of the main book, as you seek to receive your answered prayer. As you apply the elements of *Learn, Abide and Believe* to your prayer needs and pray according to God's will, watch your prayer life soar.

When you seek to "Learn" the characteristics and attributes of Jesus, read and pursue what it means to "Abide" in Him, then stand and "Believe" on His promises, you will confidently release your faith to see your prayer answered according to His will and timing—no matter what crisis or trials arise.

Lab Journal Features

- A place to write a daily prayer request or need for a loved one, a friend, your community, the world, and more. An example is included on how to pray the Scripture, apply it, then speak or confess it.

- A place to post your responses to "A Reflective of the Soul" located at the end of each chapter in the main book.

- A place to write a prayer to various prayer focuses.

- A place to write answered prayers and a description of the outcome.

- A place to write your response to thought-provoking questions that will reinforce the prayer principles found throughout the paperback.

- A mini guide to the power of fasting.

1
PRAYER LAB REFRESHER

THE THREE ELEMENTS: "**Learn, Abide, and Believe**" will help you to experience a wonderful guide in how we pray and receive answers to our prayers. I introduced the Prayer LAB in the main book *The Power of Relentless Prayer and Resilient Faith*. Let's take a moment to refresh our minds and build our spirits as we begin to engage the three elements throughout this journal.

LEARN HIM

Set aside time to develop a mini Bible study to search Scripture and LEARN about the character, attributes of Jesus and His way of doing things. The information you obtain will increase your faith to believe that He is the "same yesterday, and today, and forever" (Hebrews 13:8).

Listed below are a few scriptures that will assist you in your start. You can add more as you study the Word. Be sure to write down your comments or additional scriptures you find. They will give you the assurance that the Master can and will answer your prayer according to His timing and will.

- Mark 6:56
- Acts 10:38
- Luke 9:6
- Matthew 9:35
- Matthew 4:23

List other scriptures you discover here:

_____
_____
_____
_____
_____
_____
_____

What else are you discovering about Jesus as you study?

_____
_____
_____

ABIDE IN HIM

Search for scriptures that illustrate how we as Jesus's disciples can "abide in Him, and His words abide in you, ye shall ask what ye will, and it shall be done unto you" (John 15:7). Remember, the key is to stay connected and close to the vine who is Jesus Christ as we the believers are the branches.

Be sure to write down your comments or additional scriptures you find. They will give you the assurance that the Master can and will answer your prayer according to His timing and will.

- John 15:4-27
- Revelation 1:8

List other scriptures you discover here:

_____
_____
_____
_____
_____
_____
_____

What else are you discovering about abiding in Christ as you study?

_____

_____

_____

BELIEVE HIM

Search for scriptures that illustrate how we can gain understanding by reading passages about the "heroes of faith" and listening to the men and women of God who teach the word of faith.

Romans 10:17 reads, "So then faith cometh by hearing, and hearing by the word of God." Be sure to write down your comments or additional scriptures you find. They will give you the assurance that the Master can and will answer your prayer according to His timing and will.

- John 4:48
- John 10:38
- John 14:1
- John 14:12

List other scriptures you discover here:

_____

_____

_____
_____
_____
_____

What else are you discovering about believing God as you study?

_____
_____
_____

2
PRAYER REQUESTS

As you begin to seek the Lord about the pressing issues and concerns in your world and community, He welcomes all your prayers. Whether they are focused on you, others, your community, or various situations or matters around the world, what concerns you concerns Him.

Use the following pages to write out your prayer requests one by one following this format:

1. Be specific (do not ask amiss): James 4:3 says, "Ye ask and receive not, because ye ask amiss, that ye may consume it upon your lusts." Do not ask if it would not be in God's will.

2. Find a Scripture promise for your prayer request and write it on the lines provided. Example: If you are praying for a family in need of food and housing, one Scripture promise could be Psalm 23:1.

3. Confess the promise in writing on the lines provided. Take this confession with

you throughout the day or whenever the Holy Spirit brings your request to mind. For example, "Lord, Psalm 23:1 says that you are OUR shepherd and [INSERT FAMILY NAME] shall not want or lack. In Jesus's name, amen."

4. Finally, use the prompts in the Waiting Room section to build faith and expectancy as well as to center your focus for each prayer request on learning, abiding, or believing—the three elements of Prayer LAB.

Repeat these steps for each prayer request you include in this journal. Then when God answers the request, go to the section titled Answered Prayers on pages 86–93 and write the date and description of the outcome on the lines provided.

Prayer Request

TODAY'S DATE: _____

Pause: Take a moment to pray and give thanksgiving to your heavenly Father prior to writing your prayer request.

Be Specific: Who/what are you praying for?

_____

_____

Scripture Promise

_____

_____

_____

_____

Scriptural Confession

_____

_____

_____

_____

When God answers this request, go to the section titled Answered Prayers on pages 86–93 and write the date and description of the outcome on the lines provided.

THE WAITING ROOM

While waiting for the answer, which of the three elements of Prayer LAB—learn, abide, and believe—will you need most?

_____

How will it help you to hold on and continue to be persistent?

_____

_____

Go back to chapter 5, pages 64-68 in the main book *The Power of Relentless Praying and Resilient Faith* to read the attributes and characteristics of God. Which of God's attributes speak to you as you release this prayer request?

_____

_____

How would you apply one or more of these attributes to what you feel about God right now as you wait?

_____

_____

How is the attribute (or attributes) building your faith to believe God for the answer?

_____

_____

Prayer Request

TODAY'S DATE: _____

Pause: Take a moment to pray and give thanksgiving to your heavenly Father prior to writing your prayer request.

Be Specific: Who/what are you praying for?

_____

_____

Scripture Promise

_____

_____

_____

_____

Scriptural Confession

_____

_____

_____

_____

When God answers this request, go to the section titled Answered Prayers on pages 86–93 and write the date and description of the outcome on the lines provided.

THE WAITING ROOM

While waiting for the answer, which of the three elements of Prayer LAB—learn, abide, and believe—will you need most?

_____

How will it help you to hold on and continue to be persistent?

_____

_____

Go back to chapter 5, pages 64-68 in the main book *The Power of Relentless Praying and Resilient Faith* to read the attributes and characteristics of God. Which of God's attributes speak to you as you release this prayer request?

_____

How would you apply one or more of these attributes to what you feel about God right now as you wait?

_____

_____

How is the attribute (or attributes) building your faith to believe God for the answer?

_____

_____

Prayer Request

TODAY'S DATE: _____

Pause: Take a moment to pray and give thanksgiving to your heavenly Father prior to writing your prayer request.

Be Specific: Who/what are you praying for?

_____

_____

Scripture Promise

_____

_____

_____

_____

Scriptural Confession

_____

_____

_____

_____

When God answers this request, go to the section titled Answered Prayers on pages 86–93 and write the date and description of the outcome on the lines provided.

Prayer Requests

THE WAITING ROOM

While waiting for the answer, which of the three elements of Prayer LAB—learn, abide, and believe—will you need most?

How will it help you to hold on and continue to be persistent?

Go back to chapter 5, pages 64-68 in the main book *The Power of Relentless Praying and Resilient Faith* to read the attributes and characteristics of God. Which of God's attributes speak to you as you release this prayer request?

How would you apply one or more of these attributes to what you feel about God right now as you wait?

How is the attribute (or attributes) building your faith to believe God for the answer?

Prayer Request

TODAY'S DATE: _____

Pause: Take a moment to pray and give thanksgiving to your heavenly Father prior to writing your prayer request.

Be Specific: Who/what are you praying for?

_____

_____

Scripture Promise

_____

_____

_____

_____

Scriptural Confession

_____

_____

_____

_____

When God answers this request, go to the section titled Answered Prayers on pages 86–93 and write the date and description of the outcome on the lines provided.

THE WAITING ROOM

While waiting for the answer, which of the three elements of Prayer LAB—learn, abide, and believe—will you need most?

___

How will it help you to hold on and continue to be persistent?

___

___

Go back to chapter 5, pages 64-68 in the main book *The Power of Relentless Praying and Resilient Faith* to read the attributes and characteristics of God. Which of God's attributes speak to you as you release this prayer request?

___

___

How would you apply one or more of these attributes to what you feel about God right now as you wait?

___

___

How is the attribute (or attributes) building your faith to believe God for the answer?

___

___

Prayer Request

TODAY'S DATE: _____

Pause: Take a moment to pray and give thanksgiving to your heavenly Father prior to writing your prayer request.

Be Specific: Who/what are you praying for?

_____

_____

Scripture Promise

_____

_____

_____

Scriptural Confession

_____

_____

_____

_____

When God answers this request, go to the section titled Answered Prayers on pages 86–93 and write the date and description of the outcome on the lines provided.

THE WAITING ROOM

While waiting for the answer, which of the three elements of Prayer LAB—learn, abide, and believe—will you need most?

_____

How will it help you to hold on and continue to be persistent?

_____

_____

Go back to chapter 5, pages 64-68 in the main book *The Power of Relentless Praying and Resilient Faith* to read the attributes and characteristics of God. Which of God's attributes speak to you as you release this prayer request?

_____

_____

How would you apply one or more of these attributes to what you feel about God right now as you wait?

_____

_____

How is the attribute (or attributes) building your faith to believe God for the answer?

_____

_____

Prayer Request

TODAY'S DATE: _____

Pause: Take a moment to pray and give thanksgiving to your heavenly Father prior to writing your prayer request.

Be Specific: Who/what are you praying for?

_____

_____

Scripture Promise

_____

_____

_____

_____

Scriptural Confession

_____

_____

_____

_____

When God answers this request, go to the section titled Answered Prayers on pages 86–93 and write the date and description of the outcome on the lines provided.

Prayer Requests

THE WAITING ROOM

While waiting for the answer, which of the three elements of Prayer LAB—learn, abide, and believe—will you need most?

How will it help you to hold on and continue to be persistent?

Go back to chapter 5, pages 64-68 in the main book *The Power of Relentless Praying and Resilient Faith* to read the attributes and characteristics of God. Which of God's attributes speak to you as you release this prayer request?

How would you apply one or more of these attributes to what you feel about God right now as you wait?

How is the attribute (or attributes) building your faith to believe God for the answer?

Prayer LAB Journal

Prayer Request

TODAY'S DATE: _____

Pause: Take a moment to pray and give thanksgiving to your heavenly Father prior to writing your prayer request.

Be Specific: Who/what are you praying for?

_____
_____

Scripture Promise

_____
_____
_____
_____

Scriptural Confession

_____
_____
_____
_____

When God answers this request, go to the section titled Answered Prayers on pages **86–93** and write the date and description of the outcome on the lines provided.

THE WAITING ROOM

While waiting for the answer, which of the three elements of Prayer LAB—learn, abide, and believe—will you need most?

_____

How will it help you to hold on and continue to be persistent?

_____

_____

_____

Go back to chapter 5, pages 64-68 in the main book *The Power of Relentless Praying and Resilient Faith* to read the attributes and characteristics of God. Which of God's attributes speak to you as you release this prayer request?

_____

_____

How would you apply one or more of these attributes to what you feel about God right now as you wait?

_____

_____

How is the attribute (or attributes) building your faith to believe God for the answer?

_____

_____

Prayer Request

TODAY'S DATE: _____

Pause: Take a moment to pray and give thanksgiving to your heavenly Father prior to writing your prayer request.

Be Specific: Who/what are you praying for?

_____

_____

Scripture Promise

_____

_____

_____

_____

Scriptural Confession

_____

_____

_____

_____

When God answers this request, go to the section titled Answered Prayers on pages 86–93 and write the date and description of the outcome on the lines provided.

The Waiting Room

While waiting for the answer, which of the three elements of Prayer LAB—learn, abide, and believe—will you need most?

_____

How will it help you to hold on and continue to be persistent?

_____

_____

_____

Go back to chapter 5, pages 64-68 in the main book *The Power of Relentless Praying and Resilient Faith* to read the attributes and characteristics of God. Which of God's attributes speak to you as you release this prayer request?

_____

_____

How would you apply one or more of these attributes to what you feel about God right now as you wait?

_____

_____

How is the attribute (or attributes) building your faith to believe God for the answer?

_____

_____

Prayer Request

TODAY'S DATE: _____

Pause: Take a moment to pray and give thanksgiving to your heavenly Father prior to writing your prayer request.

Be Specific: Who/what are you praying for?

_____

_____

Scripture Promise

_____

_____

_____

Scriptural Confession

_____

_____

_____

_____

When God answers this request, go to the section titled Answered Prayers on pages 86–93 and write the date and description of the outcome on the lines provided.

Prayer Requests

THE WAITING ROOM

While waiting for the answer, which of the three elements of Prayer LAB—learn, abide, and believe—will you need most?

_____

How will it help you to hold on and continue to be persistent?

_____

_____

_____

Go back to chapter 5, pages 64-68 in the main book *The Power of Relentless Praying and Resilient Faith* to read the attributes and characteristics of God. Which of God's attributes speak to you as you release this prayer request?

_____

_____

How would you apply one or more of these attributes to what you feel about God right now as you wait?

_____

_____

How is the attribute (or attributes) building your faith to believe God for the answer?

_____

_____

Prayer Request

TODAY'S DATE: _____

Pause: Take a moment to pray and give thanksgiving to your heavenly Father prior to writing your prayer request.

Be Specific: Who/what are you praying for?

_____

_____

Scripture Promise

_____

_____

_____

Scriptural Confession

_____

_____

_____

_____

When God answers this request, go to the section titled Answered Prayers on pages 86–93 and write the date and description of the outcome on the lines provided.

The Waiting Room

While waiting for the answer, which of the three elements of Prayer LAB—learn, abide, and believe—will you need most?

_____

How will it help you to hold on and continue to be persistent?

_____

_____

Go back to chapter 5, pages 64-68 in the main book *The Power of Relentless Praying and Resilient Faith* to read the attributes and characteristics of God. Which of God's attributes speak to you as you release this prayer request?

_____

How would you apply one or more of these attributes to what you feel about God right now as you wait?

_____

_____

How is the attribute (or attributes) building your faith to believe God for the answer?

_____

_____

PRAYER LAB JOURNAL

PRAYER REQUEST

TODAY'S DATE: _____

Pause: Take a moment to pray and give thanksgiving to your heavenly Father prior to writing your prayer request.

Be Specific: Who/what are you praying for?

_____

_____

Scripture Promise

_____

_____

_____

Scriptural Confession

_____

_____

_____

When God answers this request, go to the section titled Answered Prayers on pages 86–93 and write the date and description of the outcome on the lines provided.

The Waiting Room

While waiting for the answer, which of the three elements of Prayer LAB—learn, abide, and believe—will you need most?

_____

How will it help you to hold on and continue to be persistent?

_____

_____

Go back to chapter 5, pages 64-68 in the main book *The Power of Relentless Praying and Resilient Faith* to read the attributes and characteristics of God. Which of God's attributes speak to you as you release this prayer request?

_____

_____

How would you apply one or more of these attributes to what you feel about God right now as you wait?

_____

_____

How is the attribute (or attributes) building your faith to believe God for the answer?

_____

_____

Prayer Request

TODAY'S DATE: _____

Pause: Take a moment to pray and give thanksgiving to your heavenly Father prior to writing your prayer request.

Be Specific: Who/what are you praying for?

_____

_____

Scripture Promise

_____

_____

_____

_____

Scriptural Confession

_____

_____

_____

_____

When God answers this request, go to the section titled Answered Prayers on pages 86–93 and write the date and description of the outcome on the lines provided.

THE WAITING ROOM

While waiting for the answer, which of the three elements of Prayer LAB—learn, abide, and believe—will you need most?

___

How will it help you to hold on and continue to be persistent?

___

___

___

Go back to chapter 5, pages 64-68 in the main book *The Power of Relentless Praying and Resilient Faith* to read the attributes and characteristics of God. Which of God's attributes speak to you as you release this prayer request?

___

___

How would you apply one or more of these attributes to what you feel about God right now as you wait?

___

___

How is the attribute (or attributes) building your faith to believe God for the answer?

___

___

3
GUIDED PRAYER FOCUSES

THERE ARE TIMES when we feel a burden to pray but may not know where to start or what to say. On the next few pages, I've provided some guided prayers and prayer prompts to help you release those prayer burdens to the Lord, to approach His throne boldly in times of need. You will find a prayer prompt covering the following subjects:

- Prayer for those in authority
- Prayer for widows, the poor, and orphans
- Prayer for spiritual leaders
- Prayer of thanksgiving
- Prayer for my children and grandchildren
- Prayer of expectancy
- Prayer when the answer is no
- Prayer for unity and love to prevail
- Prayer for the incarcerated and those with addictions

Guided Prayer Focuses

- Prayer for physical and emotional healing
- Prayer for salvation and restoration
- Prayer for those who are single
- Prayer for those who have suffered loss

After reading the prompts, personalize your prayers by writing them in your own words on the lines provided. You will also see that I left room for you to write your own prayer prompt and corresponding prayer.

Travail and intercede for these needs.

- Travail: to cry out in the spirit and sometimes physically on their behalf.

- Intercede: to stand in faith with someone through an "enact of partnership agreement" found in chapter 6, page 88 of *The Power of Relentless Prayer and Resilient Faith*.

Prayer for Those in Authority

In chapter 2 of *The Power of Relentless Prayer and Resilient Faith*, the unjust judge is the second main character of this thirty-ninth parable and plays a vital role in resolving the issue with the defenseless widow. However, his character is portrayed as unkind and downright rude. Even in our times, when we may see people who are in positions of authority who serve us on a daily basis behave badly, it is still important that we pray for them.

First Timothy 2:1-2 says, "I exhort therefore, that, first of all, supplications, prayers, intercessions, and giving of thanks, be made for all men; for kings, and for all that are in authority; that we may lead a quiet and peaceable life in all godliness and honesty."

Take a few moments and write a short prayer for those who make major decisions on behalf of our cities, countries, and the world. As you write, remember the attributes and character of God. He loves them. Please revisit this prayer often and pray it.

_____

_____

_____

_____

Guided Prayer Focuses

Prayer for the Widows, Poor, and Orphans

We understand that God has a special place in His heart for widows, the poor, and orphans. (See Exodus 22:22-23 and Zechariah 7:10.) These individuals are under His providential care; therefore, we should pray for them and see that resources be provided for them.

Take a few moments and write a prayer for those who are less fortunate, homeless, or in need within your city, nation, and world. Be sure to remember the Master's attributes and character as you write.

_____
_____
_____
_____
_____
_____
_____
_____
_____
_____
_____
_____

Guided Prayer Focuses

Prayer for Spiritual Leaders

Jeremiah 3:15 reads, "And I will give you pastors according to mine heart, which shall feed you with knowledge and understanding." Write a prayer for our spiritual leaders who guide us at the place where we worship.

In today's times, the role of the leader is being tested and sifted. Together, we can intercede, travail, and cry out for their strength and endurance. Remember, the attributes and character of God as you write this prayer.

_____

_____

_____

_____

_____

_____

_____

_____

_____

_____

_____

_____

_____

_____

Guided Prayer Focuses

PRAYER FOR MY CHILDREN AND GRANDCHILDREN

There is no one who loves your children and grandchildren—both natural and spiritual—more than our heavenly Father. (See Psalm 127:3; 132:12.) He has entrusted them to you (us) to protect, guide, and nurture. At times, they will test you and you may feel there is no more you can do. When that season occurs, you must reach up and pull on your faith; ask God for wisdom to carry you through.

Write a short prayer to ask Him for help. Share with Him the challenges you are experiencing as a parent, grandparent, or guardian.

Began to speak life into their future and their goals, dreams, and aspirations. Include your young adults in this prayer too.

Blessings to you in your journey of parenting.

_____
_____
_____
_____
_____
_____
_____
_____
_____

Guided Prayer Focuses

Prayer of Expectancy

Expectancy and waiting are somewhat connected. You may feel like giving up but continue to pursue until the answer is manifested or comes to pass. Continue to pray relentlessly. Trust God!

Write a prayer to ask for the Master's help if you are overwhelmed or you have been waiting a long time. He will answer according to His will and timing. May God's peace abide with you.

_____
_____
_____
_____
_____
_____
_____
_____
_____
_____
_____
_____
_____
_____
_____
_____

Guided Prayer Focuses

A Prayer When the Answer Is No

What do you do when you've prayed for something and the answer is no? At that moment, you may experience many things. You may become numb. Remember, you have prayed, cried, and fasted in expectation to receive a favorable response. (See page 79 in the main book, as well as the teaching on fasting in chapter 6.)

To our human mind, being told no is a form of rejection. I encourage you to place everything on pause and become quiet before God. Do not allow the enemy to download defeat and discouragement into your spirit. Go back and read the attributes of God in chapter 5. God knows best, and He has something better.

King David encourages us in Psalm 27:14: "Wait on the Lord: be of good courage, and he shall strengthen thine heart: wait, I say, on the Lord."

Write a letter to your heavenly Father and share your heart with Him.

_____
_____
_____
_____
_____
_____

Guided Prayer Focuses

Prayer of Unity and for Love to Prevail

This is the time to pray for the revival fires to begin and continue among our churches worldwide. Let us pray for the prodigals to return and the gospel to be preach, heard, and received around the world. Write a prayer to your heavenly Father concerning these needs. Refer to John 3:16 and John 10:16 for inspiration.

Guided Prayer Focuses

Prayer for Those Who Have Suffered Loss

(THROUGH DEATH OR RELATIONSHIP)

Have you ever experienced the loss of a loved one through death or a broken relationship? At times, the pain you feel can be unbearable. The psalmist offers God's comfort in Psalm 147:3: "He healeth the broken in heart, and bindeth up their wounds."

Write a short prayer of encouragement on behalf of yourself or someone you know who has suffered a loss and the pain remains. Include several of the attributes of the Master found in chapter 5.

_____
_____
_____
_____
_____
_____
_____
_____
_____
_____
_____
_____

Guided Prayer Focuses

PRAYER FOR THOSE WHO ARE SINGLE

In 1 Corinthians 7:34, Apostle Paul distinguishes the characteristics of a married woman to the single woman: "The unmarried or single careth for the things of the Lord, that she may be holy both in body and spirit."

Are you single or know of someone who is single? May I say that you are important to the heavenly Father and a beautiful treasure in His eyes. God has placed the desire to love and be loved within you. As you wait for that special someone to come, occupy yourself by pleasing God in the assignment He has created you to do in the kingdom.

Write a prayer on behalf of a friend or loved who may be struggling with singlehood. Ask God to encourage them to remain strong and trust in Him.

_____
_____
_____
_____
_____
_____
_____
_____

Guided Prayer Focuses

Prayer of Thanksgiving

No matter what the situation looks like, there will be times when it seems that God is not working or that He has forgotten you. Yet He is behind the scenes repositioning and preparing you to receive the answer.

Write a short prayer to give Him thanks for working it out for your good. He is your heavenly Father and cares deeply for you.

Romans 8:28, "And we know that all things work together for good to them that love God, to them who are called according to his purpose."

_____
_____
_____
_____
_____
_____
_____
_____
_____
_____
_____
_____
_____

Guided Prayer Focuses

Prayer for the Incarcerated and Those with Addictions

Luke 4:18 reads, "The spirit of the Lord is upon me, because he hath anointed me to preach the gospel to the poor; he hath sent me to heal the brokenhearted, to preach deliverance to the captive, and recovering of sight to the blind, to set at liberty them that are bruised."

Write a prayer for strongholds to be released and those who are bound be set free that their hearts will be receptive to hear the gospel or good news of His saving grace. Pray they have a repentant spirit to accept Christ as their Lord and Savior.

_____
_____
_____
_____
_____
_____
_____
_____
_____
_____
_____
_____

Guided Prayer Focuses

Prayer for Physical and Emotional Healing

Write a prayer on behalf of family, friends, coworkers, or neighbors who needs God's healing or deliverance. (See Matthew 9:35.) Ask God to remind them that Jesus Christ is the "same yesterday, to day, and for ever" (Heb. 13:8).

Guided Prayer Focuses

Prayer for Salvation and Restoration

Write a prayer on behalf of family, friends, coworkers, neighbors, and nations who are closed to the gospel. (See 2 Peter 3:9 and Revelation 3:20.)

_____
_____
_____
_____
_____
_____
_____
_____
_____
_____
_____
_____
_____
_____
_____
_____
_____
_____

Guided Prayer Focuses

A Prayer For…

Is there a prayer on your heart that we have not listed? Please write the prayer topic or focus on the line below. Then write this need to the Master in the line provided.

Your Prayer Focus: _____

_____
_____
_____
_____
_____
_____
_____
_____
_____
_____
_____
_____
_____
_____
_____
_____
_____
_____

Guided Prayer Focuses

A Prayer For...

Is there a prayer on your heart that we have not listed? Please write the prayer topic or focus on the line below. Then write this need to the Master in the line provided.

Your Prayer Focus: _____

_____
_____
_____
_____
_____
_____
_____
_____
_____
_____
_____
_____
_____
_____
_____
_____
_____
_____

Guided Prayer Focuses

4
WHILE YOU ARE WAITING

THE WORD *TRUST* is a cousin to *belief.* While you are waiting, find another prayer intercessor who will stand with you to *enact partnership of agreement*, an action key (found in chapter 6) for the request you have asked of God.

For a moment, the widow almost gave up because it seemed like no one cared, called, or stopped by to help her. Then she reflected on a previous incident when God delivered her. Praise God!

While you wait, write a prayer to God about any fear that has gripped you. Find a scripture about your situation and remind Him of His Word. For instance, you can say, "Jesus, but you said in Your Word in 1 John 5:14-15, '...and this is the confidence we have in him, that, if we ask anything according to your will, he heareth us.'" Confess this promise daily. We must pray according to His will and timing.

_____

_____

_____

Scripture Promises to Hold on to While You Wait

Prayer

> For we have not an high priest which cannot be touched with the feeling of our infirmities; but was in all points tempted like as we are, yet without sins. Let us therefore come boldly unto the throne of grace, that we may obtain mercy, and find grace to help in time of need.
> —Hebrews 4:15-16

Forgiveness

> And when you stand praying, forgive, if ye have ought against any that your Father also which is in heaven may forgive you your trespasses.
> —Mark 11:25

Confidence/Assurance

> And this is the confidence that we have in him, that, if we ask any thing according to his will, he heareth us: And if we know

that he hear us, whatsoever we ask, we know that we have the petitions that we desired of him.
—1 John 5:14-15

Purpose/Destiny

For I know the thoughts that I think toward you, saith the Lord, thoughts of peace, and not of evil, to give you an expected end.
—Jeremiah 29:11

Trust/Faith

Then came the word of the LORD unto Jeremiah, saying, Behold, I am the LORD, the God of all flesh: is there any thing too hard for me?
—Jeremiah 32:26-27

Trust in the Lord with all thine heart; and lean not unto thine own understanding.
—Proverbs 3:5

Hope/Discouragement

Why art thou cast down, O my soul? And why art thou disquieted in me? hope thou in God: for I shall yet praise him for the help of his countenance.
—Psalm 42:5

While You Wait, Secure Your Heart with These Three Actions

1. Remember God's Attributes and His Character

Go back and visit the Prayer LAB in chapter 5. List several attributes and character of our heavenly Father below. Write in your own words what each means and how that attribute has impacted your life.

Attribute of God: _____

How has this attribute changed your life, and what does it mean to you?

_____
_____
_____
_____
_____

Attribute of God: _____

How has this attribute changed your life, and what does it mean to you?

_____
_____
_____
_____

Attribute of God: _____

How has this attribute changed your life, and what does it mean to you?

_____
_____
_____
_____
_____

Attribute of God: _____

How has this attribute changed your life, and what does it mean to you?

_____
_____
_____
_____
_____

Attribute of God: _____

How has this attribute changed your life, and what does it mean to you?

_____

_____

_____

_____

_____

2. Rest in God. He is in control!

We often use the word *rest* in terms of reclining, taking a break or a nap, or possible going to bed for the night. Let's think about how this word can be used in an even greater way. For example, have you wrestled with an impossible situation (unpaid hospital bills, house in foreclosure, unemployment, to name a few) that you do not know what to do or where to turn? This is a time to trust your heavenly Father. What does it look like for you to *rest* in God for the answer?

_____

_____

_____

_____

3. Do not give up!

In Luke 18:1, Apostle Luke pens this scripture to alert the disciples to pray always and not give up. Read this verse in your favorite Bible version.

> Does this scripture mean that we are to always be on our knees or in a posture of prayer 24/7?

How would you interpret this scripture? Please write in your own words the meaning of this scripture and how it can be applied to your prayer journey?

_____
_____
_____
_____

While You Wait, Search Your Heart

The hidden red scarf in chapter 6 symbolized the possibility of hidden sin. Do not carry hidden sin or unforgiveness. They are toxic and can hinder breakthrough in prayer.

As you wait, invite the Holy Spirit to search your heart to see if there is any sin, bitterness, or anger against anyone that would prevent your prayer from being answered. Some examples may be church hurt, a broken relationship with a loved one or family member, injustice, wrongful job termination and more.

Now write a prayer to ask God for release from what He shows you.

_____
_____

While You Wait, Stay Hopeful and Know Delayed Is not Denied

Oftentimes, we feel God does not hear us. But I want you to know He does hear you and will answer according to His will and timing. In my discussion of the Prayer LAB in chapter 5, I mention that God will answer in three ways:

- Yes
- No ("I have something better.")
- Not yet (delayed or not time)

Write a short prayer to give Him thanks for working it out for your good. He is your heavenly Father and cares deeply for you.

5
REFLECTIVE MOMENTS OF THE SOUL

Chapter 1

For a moment, visualize yourself as a student of the Master during His brief three-year teaching term. In that moment, how would you feel as you sit at Jesus's feet and listen to His final instructions prior to His departure?

In what way can you take what you have learned from the Master and become an influencer to change the world?

_____

_____

_____

_____

> And ye shall seek me, and find me, when ye shall search for me with all your heart.
> —Jeremiah 29:13

Chapter 2

Write about a time you experienced disrespect.

_____

_____

Do you still carry the scars today?

If not, how did you heal?

If you are still carrying hurt from this experience, how is God leading you to release your accuser so you can live a life of abundance and fulfill your purpose in the earth?

> And whatsoever we ask, we receive of him, because we keep his commandments, and do those things that are pleasing in his sight.
> —1 JOHN 3:22

Chapter 3

Write about a time you were ignored or made to feel insignificant.

_____
_____
_____
_____
_____
_____

In that moment, you may have reacted in three ways: you experienced hurt, became angry, or you were in denial. Injustice stinks.

As you reflect on the incident, how would you react differently now?

_____
_____

How did this experience change you? How have you moved forward or has the residue become part of the present?

_____
_____
_____
_____

Chapter 4

Write about a time when you made a bad impression and regretted it.

_____
_____
_____
_____
_____

It's never too late to try again. Do not let the ugly spirit of fear delay you from seizing the moment to walk in your destiny.

If given another opportunity, what would you do differently?

_____
_____
_____
_____

Chapter 5

What is that "hard thing" for which you are believing God for a breakthrough?

_____
_____
_____

Which element of LAB—learn, abide, and believe—represents the most challenging position for you to take as you wait in prayer? Write about what makes it so challenging.

_____

_____

_____

_____

For one week, take one of these elements and use its principles to apply to your prayer regarding this "hard thing."

My friend, watch the Master work. Don't forget to write the praise report in the section of this journal titled Answered Prayer.

Chapter 6

Reflect over the past five years of your life. What is the shift or transition that would have changed your life for the better if you had taken it?

_____

_____

_____

How has your decision resonated with you since then?

_____

_____

_____

_____

If you had the opportunity to go back and do it again, would you grasp the moment?

_____

_____

_____

Chapter 7

Write about a time when the answer to your prayer was delayed. How did you feel in the moments between the time you prayed and the time you received your answer?

_____

_____

_____

_____

_____

As you have matured in your journey of prayer, what, if anything, would you have done differently as you waited? Was there anything you could have done to receive an answer faster?

_____

Chapter 8

Write about a time when you experienced an emergency, and you needed a prayer to be answered immediately yet it was delayed.

Now, write about a time you prayed and the Master answered quickly.

Contrast these two experiences. What was different about you or the situations that led to how the prayers were answered?

Reflective Moments of the Soul

_____
_____
_____
_____

Finally, share with a friend what you've learned about God, yourself, and prayer through this analysis.

6
FASTING: TAKING PRAYER TO THE NEXT LEVEL

A SIMPLE DEFINITION OF fasting is to abstain or (pull back) from eating for a period of time. It is also a time of refreshing or consecration. Fasting is not by force. It is an invitation. Obey the Master when he nudges you to pull back from eating; the rewards are overwhelming.

A shepherd or pastor may call a corporate fast for his congregation to join in unity for a time of refreshing.

WHY DO WE FAST?

Isaiah 58:6 gives four reasons why we should embrace this discipline:

1. To loose the bands of wickedness
2. To undo the heavy burdens
3. To let the oppressed go free
4. To break (destroy) every yoke

What is a yoke?

A yoke is a wooden harness placed around the neck of two oxen to strengthen whatever load they are pulling. This is symbolic of the weight many believers are carrying. As intercessors, we must war in the spirit to break this harness off of those who are bound to be free to serve Christ.

FASTING REQUIRES SACRIFICE

It can be uncomfortable to the flesh. Ask yourself, What is something I love to do, eat, or go to so much that it makes it hard to give up for a period of time to spend with God? This can be things like TV, social media, and more.

PRAYER + FASTING + THE WORD = WIN

If we do not know the scriptures, we are opened to attacks from our enemy, Satan. The devil does not like it when we speak or confess God's promises back to him about a situation we face. Reading, studying, and mediating on God's Word is vital in assisting us in a victorious prayer life.

Psalm 119:105 reads, "Thy word is a lamp unto my feet, and a light unto my path."

Second Timothy 2:15 admonishes: "Do your best to present yourself to God as one approved, a worker who does not need to be ashamed and who correctly handles the word of truth" (NIV).

When we combine prayer with the discipline of fasting and speaking the Word, we can win.

EXERCISE ACTIVITY*

Before *reading* the Word, speak this affirmation.

Heavenly Father, I set myself in agreement with Your Word that I am the righteousness of God in Him that is Christ Jesus. I walk in faith and not by sight. I realize that real faith is seeing faith and is acting in confidence responding to the Word of God.

I have been given authority over all of my adversaries. I now, in the name of Jesus Christ, put all of them under my feet for they shall not by any means hurt me. I put under my feet sickness, disease, poverty, fear, depression, oppression, repression, aggression, yokes, weights, cruelty, animosity, antagonism, frustration, hostility, jealously, envying, strife, gossip, and any other things of like passion.

I pull down every stronghold, I cast down imagination and every high thing that exalts itself against the knowledge of God, and I bring into captivity every thought to the obedience

---

* The writer of this exercise acivity is anonymous. The author has search online and various worshop materials for the author's name to receive permisson and give proper acknowledgment.

of Christ. For I think of things that are pure, things of honor, things that are just, things that are true, things that are lovely, things that are a good report, things of virtue, and things of praise.

I will always rejoice in the Lord greatly. I will lack nothing for I am Christ sufficient. I can do all things through Christ who strengthens me. I receive all in the name of Jesus Christ. Amen. (See Philippians 3:9; 4:8, 13.)

Types of Fasting

There are various types of fasts. Some may feel the need to fast seven or twenty-one days with water while denying food. Others may do a partial fast or the plant-based Daniel fast. Be led by God about which fast is best for your body. Ask a pastor or leader of your church to pray with you before you began a lengthy fast or if you have questions about fasting. Note: If you are on medication, it is always recommended to consult with your physician before you begin any fast.

What Are the Benefits of Fasting?

1. We become more sensitive to hear God's voice to hear how He desires us to move in a particular situation.

2. We will conquer our flesh from overeating. We remind it that we will not kneel to the enemy's strategy of gluttony. Satan's plan is to "steal, kill and destroy" at any cost and to cause us to abort the assignment or mission we have been given from God (John 10:10).

3. When we fast, we witness God's deliverance and manifestation of His signs, wonders, and miracles.

Envision yourself as a student in training (His disciple), sitting and talking with Him. What two questions would you like to ask Him about prayer and fasting? Be specific.

_____

_____

For more, review fasting in chapter 6 of *The Power of Relentless Prayer and Resilient Faith*.

7
ANSWERED PRAYERS

Use the following pages to write your testimonies for the prayers God has answered according to the prayer request you wrote earlier in this journal. Include the day's date, the date you first went to God in prayer for the situation, and the date the answer came. Then freely share a description of the outcome.

Prayer LAB Journal

ANSWERED PRAYER

Today's date: _____

Date of original prayer request: _____

Date the answer came: _____

How did God answer? Be specific.

_____
_____
_____
_____
_____
_____
_____
_____
_____
_____
_____
_____
_____
_____
_____
_____
_____
_____
_____

ANSWERED PRAYER

Today's date: _____

Date of original prayer request: _____

Date the answer came: _____

How did God answer? Be specific.

_____
_____
_____
_____
_____
_____
_____
_____
_____
_____
_____
_____
_____
_____
_____
_____

Prayer LAB Journal

ANSWERED PRAYER

Today's date: _____

Date of original prayer request: _____

Date the answer came: _____

How did God answer? Be specific.

_____
_____
_____
_____
_____
_____
_____
_____
_____
_____
_____
_____
_____
_____
_____
_____

ANSWERED PRAYER

Today's date: _____

Date of original prayer request: _____

Date the answer came: _____

How did God answer? Be specific.

Prayer LAB Journal

ANSWERED PRAYER

Today's date: _____

Date of original prayer request: _____

Date the answer came: _____

How did God answer? Be specific.

_____
_____
_____
_____
_____
_____
_____
_____
_____
_____
_____
_____
_____
_____
_____
_____
_____
_____
_____

ANSWERED PRAYER

Today's date: _____

Date of original prayer request: _____

Date the answer came: _____

How did God answer? Be specific.

_____
_____
_____
_____
_____
_____
_____
_____
_____
_____
_____
_____
_____
_____
_____
_____
_____
_____
_____
_____

Prayer LAB Journal

ANSWERED PRAYER

Today's date: _____

Date of original prayer request: _____

Date the answer came: _____

How did God answer? Be specific.

_____
_____
_____
_____
_____
_____
_____
_____
_____
_____
_____
_____
_____
_____
_____
_____
_____

ANSWERED PRAYER

Today's date: _____

Date of original prayer request: _____

Date the answer came: _____

How did God answer? Be specific.

_____
_____
_____
_____
_____
_____
_____
_____
_____
_____
_____
_____
_____
_____
_____
_____
_____
_____

Prayer LAB Journal

NOTES

NOTES

NOTES

NOTES

NOTES

NOTES

SPECIAL NOTE FROM THE AUTHOR

It is my hope that *The Power of Relentless Prayer and Resilient Faith Prayer LAB Journal* has been a blessing to you. When you begin to infuse the elements of learn, abide, and believe in your prayer life, watch God answer your prayers according to His will and timing.

I would love to hear from you. Please write and leave a review to let me know how the book *The Power of Relentless Prayer and Resilient Faith* and the *Prayer LAB Journal* helped you in your prayer journey. My contact information is listed on the back page of this journal.

Blessings,
Doris E. Golder

Other Books by Doris E. Golder

Gifts of Grace: Seven Keys to Discover Your Hidden Potential

The Power of Relentless Prayer and Resilient Faith

CONTACT INFORMATION

doris@dvinestrategies.com
www.dvinestrategies.com

www.ingramcontent.com/pod-product-compliance
Lightning Source LLC
Chambersburg PA
CBHW061738070526
44585CB00024B/2731